# The Cozy Queen Cookbook

## Volume One

Copyright 2025 Julie Hatcher

All rights reserved. This book or any portion thereof
may not be reproduced or used in any manner whatsoever
without the express written consent of the publisher. Except for
the use of brief quotations in a book review.

Printed by Cozy Queen Publishing, in the United States of America

First printing 2025
978-1-954878-44-0

Cozy Queen Publishing
Kent, Ohio, USA

julieannelindsey.com

To the Cozy Queens
You make my dream possible
(and delicious!)

# Table of Contents

| | |
|---|---|
| A Note From the Author | 1 |
| Kitchen Tips & Tricks from Cozy Queens | 2 |
| Cider Shop Collection | 5 |
| Kitchen Tips & Tricks from Cozy Queens | 15 |
| Seaside Cafe Collection | 18 |
| Kitchen Tips & Tricks from Cozy Queens | 25 |
| Recipes from My House | 28 |
| Kitchen Tips & Tricks from Cozy Queens | 35 |
| Christmas Tree Farm Collection | 41 |
| Kitchen Tips & Tricks from Cozy Queens | 46 |
| Kitty Couture Collection | 48 |
| Kitchen Tips & Tricks from Cozy Queens | 55 |
| Bonnie & Clyde Collection | 57 |
| Kitchen Tips & Tricks from Cozy Queens | 64 |
| Thelma & Louisa Collection | 66 |
| Kitchen Tips & Tricks from Cozy Queens | 71 |
| Acknowledgements | 73 |

# A NOTE FROM THE AUTHOR

Hello, Lovely Reader!

It's me, Julie Anne Hatcher, though some of you might know me as Julie Anne Lindsey, Bree Baker, Jacqueline Frost or Julie Chase.

Regardless of how you know me, our shared love of cozy mysteries has already made us friends. And my friends LOVE cozy mystery recipes, which is why I've created THE COZY QUEEN COOKBOOK, and THE COZY QUEEN COOKBOOK Volume 1!

THE COZY QUEEN COOKBOOK Volume 1 contains recipes inspired by my many cozy mystery series, including the Seaside Café Mysteries, Cider Shop Mysteries, Kitty Couture Mysteries, Christmas Tree Farm Mysteries, Bonnie & Clyde Mysteries, Thelma & Louisa Mysteries!

I've even included bonus recipes from my home to yours and numerous kitchen tips and tricks sent in by my Cozy Queens, readers and friends!

HUGE & sincere thanks to each of you for making this cookbook and my dream possible. I mean that from the bottom of my heart and batter bowl!

Julie

# Kitchen Tips & Tricks from the Cozy Queens

You'll find this section repeated throughout the book. I asked my fellow cozy mystery readers, fans, and friends to share things they do in their kitchens to make life easier and more delicious.
They did not disappoint!
As you read, I hope you'll see a few tips you already know and find camaraderie on the pages.
I also hope you'll come across a few new ideas and find value in the content.

### Jenny Baked Goodies

"If I bake cookies and someone forgot to close the lid on the storage container, or if it's been a few days and they are loosing their moistness, I ball up a couple pieces of white bread and add them to the container to keep the cookies tasting like day one. I also do this when I ship cookies to people."

# Kitchen Tips & Tricks from the Cozy Queens

### Reba A.

"If baking a chocolate cake, I use cocoa to dust the cake pan instead of white flour."

"Use frozen, grated butter for fluffy pastry or mashed potatoes."

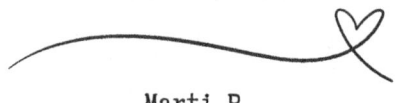

### Marti R.

"Preheat pans in the oven before putting them in cold. If the pans shift & warp, the contents might slip and mash together."

"Put plain dry rice into salt shakers to prevent caking in humid conditions."

"Butter burns, margarine doesn't but it might change the taste."

"Knives stay sharper longer if you wash and dry them immediately after use."

# Kitchen Tips & Tricks from the Cozy Queens

### Neva L.
"When a recipe calls for adding dry ingredients to wet ingredients, I put the dry ingredients onto wax paper and add to mixer. Using wax paper makes it easier to add without any mess."

### Kirsty G.
"I convert my baking recipes to weights. Especially with flour, this eliminates the differences due to how packed it is."

### Jean G.
"If your family doesn't like bits of onion in their sauces, put a whole peeled onion in to cook, then remove it before serving."

# And Now

## Recipes inspired by: CIDER SHOP COLLECTION

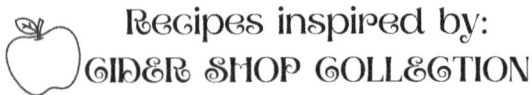

Welcome to Blossom Valley, West Virginia, a small farming community nestled in the heart of the Blue Ridge Mountains. Winnie Mae Montgomery is busy running her new cider shop from the historic Mail Pouch barn on her family's property. Her Granny Smythe is taking care of the orchard and local folks any way she can.

Stop by anytime, sit a spell and sample Winnie's cider. Learn about the long history and unwavering community spirit of their town, or maybe join Winnie in her meddling. She sure does love to help the Sheriff with his investigations. Even when he hasn't asked. Maybe especially then.

*

The following recipes were inspired by
The Cider Shop Mysteries by Julie Anne Lindsey
APPLE CIDER SLAYING
PULP FRICTION
THE CIDER SHOP RULES

# Beef Stew
Hearty, old-fashioned, stick-to-your-ribs Good!

**INGREDIENTS**
- 2lbs chuck roast
- 1 shallot
- 1 onion
- 1 carrot
- 2 celery sticks
- 8oz mushrooms
- 2 bay leaves
- 1tsp worchestershire sauce
- 1tsp soy sauce
- ½ tsp oregano
- ½ tsp thyme
- ½ tsp savory
- 1 tsp salt
- ½ tsp black pepper
- 32oz beef stock
- 1 tsbp olive oil

**INSTRUCTIONS**
- Cut beef into 1-inch cubes. Season with salt and pepper.
- Dice vegetables; place shallot, carrot, and celery in 1 bowl, onions in 1 bowl, and mushrooms in a 3rd bowl.
- Measure out spices and place in a small dish.
- Heat oil in a covered soup pot over medium high heat. Cook beef cubes until browned. Remove beef from the pot and set aside.

*Continued on next page

## BEEF STEW Continued

- Cook the shallot, carrot, and celery until soft. Remove from pot and return to their bowl. Cover.
- Cook mushrooms until browned and return to their bowl.
- Cook onion until soft. Return meat to the pot and cover with the beef stock.
- Add bay leaves and seasonings.
- Cook over low heat for approximately 2 hours or until stock has significantly reduced.
- Add the vegetables in the covered bowl back to the pot and cook until warmed through.

# Miss Mary Ellen's Marinara Sauce

Add some down home zip to your pasta with this quick & easy recipe from Miss Mary Ellen's kitchen!

## Ingredients

- 1 pint cherry tomatoes
- 2 cloves of garlic minced
- 1 tsp Italian seasoning
- 1 pinch of salt
- 1 Tbsp butter
- 5 dashes Worcestershire sauce
- 5 dashes soy sauce

## Instructions

- Melt the butter in a saucepan over medium heat.
- Cook tomatoes in butter for 10 minutes. Add Worcestershire sauce, soy sauce, and garlic to the saucepan. Reduce heat to low. Cook until tomatoes are soft and are easily smashed with a wooden spoon.
- Add Italian seasoning and salt to taste. Continue to cook over low heat until desired consistency is reached.
- If you want smooth sauce, use am immersion blender to blend the tomatoes into a smooth consistency.

# Granny's Sweet Pickles

There is nothing sweeter than a homemade pickle, and Granny's recipe is sure to please the pickiest pickle people!

### INGREDIENTS:

- 2 medium cucumbers (sliced)
- 1 cup sugar
- ½ cup water
- ½ cup vinegar
- 1 teaspoon salt
- Dill to taste

### INSTRUCTIONS:

- Boil together sugar, water, vinegar and salt
- Pour over sliced cucumbers
- Sprinkle with dill
- Chill and serve

# Tasty Pulled Pork

Perfect for tailgating, backyard partying, and feeding a hungry crowd.

## Ingredients

- 3 – 4lbs pork shoulder
- 2 onions
- 2 bay leaves
- 1 tsp garlic powder
- 1 tsp chili powder
- 1 tsp black pepper
- 1 tsp thyme
- 1 tsp cumin
- 2 tbsp salt
- 2 tbsp apple cider vinegar
- 32 oz chicken stock

## Instructions

- Cut pork into large cubes
- Cut onion into chunks.
- Place pork and onion into a large slow cooker
- Cover with the chicken stock and mix in all remaining ingredients.
- Cook on high for 4 hours or low for 8 hours.
- To crisp the pork, remove it from the slow cooker and place onto a rimmed baking sheet. Add some chicken stock to prevent drying out. Broil to desired texture
- Otherwise, remove pork from slow cooker and store in an airtight container.
- Mix with BBQ sauce for sandwiches.
- Also delicious over salad or in tortilla shells

# Roasted Red Pepper Triangles

Winnie's go-to recipe for sharing.
Sensational, Savory, Yum!

**INGREDIENTS:**
- 2 tubes (8 ounces each) refrigerated crescent rolls
- 1 ½ cups fully cooked ham (finely diced)
- 4 ounces shredded Swiss cheese
- 1 package (3 ounces) sliced pepperoni (chopped)
- 8 slices provolone cheese
- 1 jar (12 ounces) roasted red peppers (well drained and cut into thin strips)
- 4 eggs
- ¼ cup grated parmesan cheese
- 3 teaspoons Italian salad dressing mix

**INSTRUCTIONS:**
- Preheat oven to 350 degrees
- Prepare a of 9x13x2" baking dish with nonstick cooking spray
- Unroll one tube of crescent rolls into long rectangle and press into bottom and up the sides of pan
- Seal seams and perforations
- Top with half the ham
- Layer with Swiss cheese, pepperoni, provolone, and remaining ham
- Top with red peppers
- In a small bowl, whisk the eggs, Parmesan cheese and salad dressing mix
- Set aside ¼ cup
- Pour remaining egg mixture over peppers.
- On a lightly floured surface, roll out remaining crescent dough into a 9x13" rectangle

*Continued

# Roasted Red Pepper Triangles Continued:

- Seal seams and perforations
- Place over filling and pinch edges to seal
- Cover and bake 30 minutes
- Uncover and brush with ¼ cup egg mixture
- Bake 20 – 25 minutes longer or until crust is golden brown
- Cool on a wire rack for 5 minutes
- Cut into triangles
- Serve warm with marinara sauce for dipping

- In a small bowl, whisk the eggs, Parmesan cheese and salad dressing mix
- Set aside ¼ cup
- Pour remaining egg mixture over peppers.
- On a lightly floured surface, roll out remaining crescent dough into a 9x13" rectangle
- Seal seams and perforations
- Place over filling and pinch edges to seal
- Cover and bake 30 minutes
- Uncover and brush with ¼ cup egg mixture
- Bake 20 – 25 minutes longer or until crust is golden brown
- Cool on a wire rack for 5 minutes
- Cut into triangles
- Serve warm with marinara sauce for dipping

# Smythe's Seasonal Apple Bread

There are endless ways to enjoy apples from the orchard, but this sweet treat is perfect anytime of year!

## INGREDIENTS:

### BREAD:
- 3 cups apples diced – or applesauce
- 3 cups flour
- 2 cups sugar
- 1 cup chopped walnuts
- ½ cup vegetable oil
- 3 eggs
- 2 Tablespoons baking soda
- 1 teaspoon salt
- 1 teaspoon vanilla

### GLAZE:
- 1 stick butter
- 1 cup sugar
- ½ cup evaporated milk

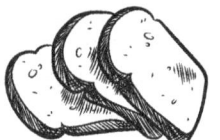

## INSTRUCTIONS:

### BREAD:
- Preheat oven to 350 degrees
- Grease and flour 2 8x4 loaf pans
- Mix oil, eggs, and sugar in a medium bowl
- Add all other ingredients and blend
- Pour mixture into pans
- Bake 90 minutes

Continued

# Apple Bread Continued

**GLAZE:**
- Heat butter, sugar, and evaporated milk in a sauce pan until boiling
- Remove from heat
- Pour over baked bread
- Cool. Slice and serve.

# Kitchen Tips & Tricks from the Cozy Queens

### Rachel J.
"I add cinnamon to the pancake mix, kids love it."

"When making a potato in the microwave, I poke holes in it then wrap each one in a wet paper towel. They're best on the grill with olive oil and in aluminum foil."

"Corn starch is so much better than flour in gravies."

### Ruby G.
"When I'm measuring something sticky like honey or molasses, I spray my cup or spoon with Pam first. So much easier to get it out of the cup and clean up."

### Cinda U.
"When making deviled eggs, I add the yolks to a large sealable bag along with the mayo and all the other ingredients. I smoosh them all together until smooth. Cut one corner tip off then pipe the filling into the eggs."

# Kitchen Tips & Tricks from the Cozy Queens

### Laura S.

Vanilla: "When opening a new bottle of vanilla, poke holes in the foil seal and leave it on. This keeps it from pouring out too quickly and you from wasting expensive vanilla."

Cooking oil: "Fill a spray bottle from the store halfway. Use this instead of nonstick spray that is chemical based."

"For fluffy scrambled eggs, add a quarter teaspoon of vinegar. It's such a small amount you won't event taste it!"

Cream Cheese mixing: "Use a mixer for blending room temp cream cheese. It's never soft enough to blend by hand."

Expiration dates: "I love those Oxo clear canisters {especially living in the country}. So when it comes time to refill with new items, take a strip of Washi tape and write the expiration date on it and tape it to the top of the lid. The tape is light adhesive so it won't stick too hard and damage the lid when it time for an update."

# Kitchen Tips & Tricks from the Cozy Queens

### Jane Ann T.

"Use frozen chopped onions instead of chopping your own."

---

"If you've burned a pan, or food is stuck to it, lay a dryer sheet on its surface and put enough warm water just to soak the dryer sheet. Let it sit for a while, and the pan will come clean."

### Reba A.

"When I'm baking cookies I place the flour, salt, baking soda, *etc in a gallon bag then seal it and thoroughly shake it to sift together everything. Then I add the contents slowly to the creamed mixture in the bowl."

# And Now

## Recipes inspired by SEASIDE CAFÉ COLLECTION

Welcome to Charm, North Carolina, an idyllic seaside town where Everly Swan's iced tea shop, Sun, Sand & Tea, overlooks the beach! You can catch Everly serving up 20 flavors of iced tea, along with her family's recipes and heaping helpings of good old fashioned southern charm, seven days a week from lunch until dinner.

Swing by and enjoy the views, listen to the gossip, and weigh in on what matters most. Her family's alleged curses? The man who's fast stealing her heart? Or Lou, the seagull keeping watch over it all?

You might even solve a local murder or two while you're there.

*

### The Seaside Café Mysteries by Bree Baker

LIVE & LET CHAI
NO GOOD TEA GOES UNPUNISHED
TIDE & PUNISHMENT
A CALL FOR KELP
CLOSELY HARBORED SECRETS
PARTNERS IN LIME
PLEADING THE FISH

## Caprese Crustini

Light on effort, BIG on taste! Make this fast, flavorful, finger food for your next luncheon or party!

### INGREDIENTS
- Baguette, sliced
- olive oil for brushing
- Pesto
- Tomatoes
- Buffalo Mozzarella
- Fresh Basil
- Balsamic Glaze
- Pine nuts, toasted

### INSTRUCTIONS
- Cut baguette into slices, brush with olive oil and grill or place on baking sheet to toast in oven.
- Spread pesto on each slice.
- Top with 1 slice each tomato and fresh mozzarella
- add basil.
- Drizzle balsamic glaze over top*
- Sprinkle with  pine nuts.

## Cucumber Cups

Need a cute, but quick appetizer? Try this finger-friendly hit!

### INGREDIENTS

- 3-4 large cucumbers
- hummus of choice
- garnish of choice (ex: paprika, fresh chives, diced bell peppers, parsley, let your taste buds decide!)

### INSTRUCTIONS

- Peel the cucumbers partially, leaving thin strips of skin that run the entire length of the cucumber
- Cut off and discard the ends of the cucumbers
- Slice each cucumber into 1-inch thick chunks
- Scoop out the center of each slice with a melon baller (leave a lining on the bottom for the filling to sit on)
- Add hummus to a pastry bag and pipe it into the cucumber cups
- Garnish and serve

Tip: Running a fork or zester down the cucumber's side can also create a cool pattern.

# Easy Stuffed Sweet Peppers
A Sun, Sand, & Tea favorite

### INGREDIENTS
- 1 cup cottage cheese
- 1 ripe avocado, diced
- 1 Green Onion, thinly sliced
- 1 tsp. garlic powder
- salt and pepper to taste
- 2 dozen sweet mini peppers

### Instructions
- Stir together avocado, cottage cheese, onion, and garlic. Add salt and pepper to taste.
- Cut off the tops of the mini peppers and remove the seeds and ribs.
- Stuff the peppers with the cottage cheese mixture.
- Chill and serve

# Greek Salad Skewer Appetizers

These veggie skewers are flavor packed, easy to make, and look great on a serving tray. Better sneak a sample while you prep them, cause they won't last once they're served.

## INGREDIENTS

- English cucumber, cut into slices, then slices cut in half
- 8 pitted Kalamata olives, cut in half
- 8 grape tomatoes, cut in half
- feta cheese chunks
- 2 tablespoons extra virgin olive oil
- Salt and freshly ground black or mixed peppercorn pepper
- Extra-long toothpicks for appetizers

## INSTRUCTIONS

- Thread each of 16 toothpicks with a tomato, olive, piece of feta, and a cucumber slice.
- Place the skewers on a serving plate, drizzle with the olive oil, and sprinkle with a little salt.
- Grind the pepper over the skewers and serve.

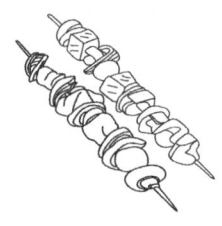

# Kalamata Olive & Goat Cheese Stuffed Cherry Tomatoes

Another pretty bite-sized treat to impress your guests and add color to your table!

### INGREDIENTS
- 24 heirloom cherry tomatoes, washed and dried
- 4 ounces goat cheese
- 1/4 cup Kalamata olives, chopped finely (optional)
- 1 tablespoon fresh oregano or basil, roughly chopped
- Freshly ground black pepper
- Dash of sea salt
- 1 tablespoon fresh chives, sliced thin

### INSTRUCTIONS
- Slice the tops off the cherry tomatoes
- Remove seeds using a small spoon
- Drain any juice
- Slice a sliver off the bottom of each tomato so it doesn't roll away
- In a bowl, mix goat cheese, Kalamata olives, fresh oregano, black pepper, and sea salt until blended
- Spoon the mixture into the tomatoes. Arrange on a serving platter, top with fresh cut chives
- Chill and serve

# Island Chicken

Need an easy and delicious way to freshen up your chicken game? This sweet and savory dish is sure to be one you'll make again and again.

INGREDIENTS:
- 3 pounds chicken
- 1 16-ounce can of crushed pineapple
- 1 cup brown sugar
- ½ cup soy sauce
- Vegetable oil for browning

INSTRUCTIONS:
- Brown chicken in a little oil
- Move browned pieces to a 9x13 baking pan
- Combine pineapple, brown sugar and soy sauce in a medium mixing bowl
- Pour over chicken
- Bake uncovered at 350 degrees for 2 hours
- Baste halfway through

# Kitchen Tips & Tricks from the Cozy Queens

### Chris L. R.
"When I make baked donuts in donut forms, I put batter in a baggie, snip off one corner and squeeze into the forms. Easier and less messy than spooning or pouring."

---

"If you are out of egg when you are baking something, you can use 1 Tablespoon of water mixed with 2 Tablespoons of ground flaxseed to make your own "egg".

---

You can also use 2-3 Tbsp of applesauce, smashed banana, or peanut butter as your egg.

---

Use applesauce in place of oil in baking recipes to add moistness and flavor.

---

If you need buttermilk or sour milk, add a splash of vinegar to your milk and let it set for a few minutes. Then voila! Sour or buttermilk.

# Kitchen Tips & Tricks from the Cozy Queens

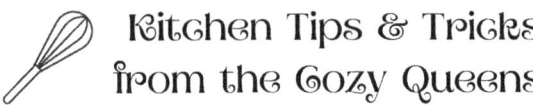

### Nicole P.

"My kitchen tip is I usually substitute plain Greek yogurt or a fruit sauce (apple, pear, etc.) in cakes and breads instead of using oil. It is so delicious, adds a new flavor dimension, keeps the baked goods super moist, and is a bit healthier than the oil! :)

### Allison Y.

"A kitchen hack I swear by is swapping out milk for sour cream when making muffins or scones. It makes them richer & fluffier. I am an avid from scratch gluten free baker, and I cannot imagine not using sour cream instead of milk these days!"

### Beth M.

When rolling out cut out cookies I dust the counter with powdered sugar instead of flour.

# Kitchen Tips & Tricks from the Cozy Queens

Marsha K. C.

"My mom always added a can of ABC veggie soup in her sloppy joes. While draining the ground beef she would put the soup in the pan and use her potato masher on the soup then add the beef and rest of the normal ingredients. (You probably could also puree the soup in a food processor.) I make mine the same way.

---

I keep a tooth brush by the kitchen sink to clean out my colander."

---

"I use vinegar to clean baked-on grime on pots and pans."

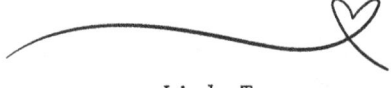

Linda T.

"If you have a recipe calling for milk or oil or dry ingredients and water at the same time, always do the water last to get that last bit of anything else that may have been left in measuring cup."

# And Now

## RECIPES FROM MY HOUSE

I'm no Everly Swan or Winnie Mae Montgomery, but I do love to treat my family with good food and sweet treats. And I always try to make things quick and easy in the kitchen.
These are just a few of my favorites recipes to make and take to parties or share with friends.
I hope one or two might find their ways into your home and heart as well.

# Stuffed Pepper Soup

Nothing brings a family together in the fall like soup and crackers. This recipe came to me many years ago, and it remains a favorite. We pack it up for potlucks, take it outside for bonfires, set it up like its own buffet with bowls of toppings and additions. I hope you'll like it as much as we do, and customize it to fit your tastes. Enjoy!

INGREDIENTS:
- 1 lb ground beef
- 2 cans diced tomatoes with chiles
- 2 cans water
- 2 beef bouillon cubes
- 1 large green pepper (diced)
- 1 red pepper (diced)
- 1 medium onion (chopped)
- 1 Tablespoon sugar
- 1 teaspoon salt

INSTRUCTIONS:
- Brown the ground been in soup pot and drain
- Add remaining ingredients and bring to a boil
- Reduce heat and stir occasionally for about an hour
- Serve with oyster crackers, a sprinkling of shredded cheese or a dollop of sour cream

# Grape Jelly Meatballs

This one's a classic and always a hit. If you don't have it, you need it. Easy peasy, three ingredients, serves a mob, and takes only a few minutes of your precious time. Break out that slow cooker!

INGREDIENTS:
- 2 12-ounce jars chili sauce
- 1 32-ounce jar of grape jelly
- 1 big bag of frozen meatballs

INSTRUCTIONS:
- Empty chili sauce and grape jelly into a slow cooker and heat until jelly is melted
- Stir until sauce is smooth
- Add frozen meatballs
- Seal the lid and forget it for about 3 hours
- Tell your guests to help themselves. You're done!

# Mama's Chocolate Rum Balls

The first time I made these, I worried the rum flavor would be lost to the chocolate, so I used 151 Rum. I sealed the container. Waited 2 days. Opened the container to take a whiff, and I think I cleared my sinuses for the next six years. Take this lesson from me: any old rum is just fine. Leave 151 for pirates and punch.

INGREDIENTS:
- 1 ½ cup of your favorite chopped nuts
- 2 cups crushed vanilla wafers
- 1 ½ cup powdered sugar
- ¼ cup cocoa powder
- 3 Tablespoons light corn syrup
- ½ cup rum

INSTRUCTIONS:
- Combine crushed wafers, sugar, cocoa powder, and nuts
- Blend in syrup and rum
- Shape into 1" balls (will be sticky)
- Roll balls in sugar
- Store in an airtight container for 1-2 days
- Roll in sugar again before serving

## Simple Baked Potatoes

I use this recipe, provided by a dear friend and reader, Robin S, when I need to feed my family lunch in a hurry. The baked potato buffet is a hit. I set out all our favorite toppings alongside the slow cooker, and they can pile them high. Easy to set up. Easy to clean up. And I don't even have to be in town while the cooking happens!

INGREDIENTS:
- Medium-sized potatoes
- Olive oil
- Salt

INSTRUCTIONS:
- Wash and dry potatoes
- Rub with olive oil
- Lightly salt
- Wrap individually in foil and stack inside the slow cooker.
- Cook on high 4 hours, or on low for 8
- *Set out a variety of toppings for your buffet and let your guests help themselves!
- Possible toppings: Butter, Sour cream, Chives, Salt & Pepper, Shredded cheese, Nacho cheese, Bacon...

# Easy Peanut Butter Fudge

This one comes from my mama, a huge fan of recipes that require minimal effort and limited ingredients, but deliver big yummy results.
Thanks, Mama!

**INGREDIENTS:**
- 2 cups of sugar
- ½ cup milk
- 1 teaspoon vanilla
- ¾ cup creamy peanut butter

**INSTRUCTIONS:**
- Add milk and sugar to a medium sauce pan and heat until roiling
- Stir constantly for 2 ½ minutes
- Remove from heat
- Add vanilla and peanut butter
- Stir until smooth
- Pour into a greased 8x8 pan
- Cool completely
- Cut and serve

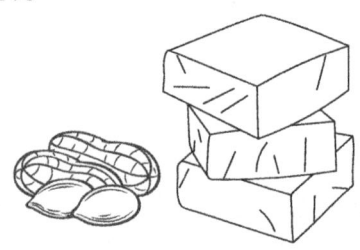

# Beef Taco Bake

It's basic. I know. Everyone has one of these recipes, but I would be remiss to leave it out. My family ate some version of this weekly when the kids were young, involved in a million things, and I was constantly on the run. Bonus: They ALL liked it - That was a miracle all by itself! And the recipe is versatile. Add your family's favorite taco toppings. It's easy and delicious!

INGREDIENTS:
- 1 lb ground beef
- 1 can condensed tomato soup
- 1 cup corn and black bean salsa
- ½ cup milk
- 6 flour tortillas, or 8 corn tortillas cut into 1-inch strips
- 1 cup shredded cheese

INSTRUCTIONS:
- Brown ground beef in a skillet over medium heat. Drain.
- Add soup, salsa, milk, tortillas, and half the cheese
- Spoon mixture into a shallow 2-Quart baking dish
- Cover and bake at 400 degrees for 30 minutes
- Sprinkle with remaining cheese

# Kitchen Tips & Tricks from the Cozy Queens

### Ceri F.
"When pounding (tenderizing) meat, put plastic wrap under and on top to prevent cross contamination."

### Traci A.
"Parchment paper! It is the best stuff ever made. Use it whenever you don't want something to stick to a pain. Cake, bacon, biscuits, most anything. But when you tear off a piece and put it on the pan it won't stay in place - until you crumple it up into a ball and then straighten it out. Then it stays perfectly!"

### Jen C.
"When making brownies, if the recipe calls for oil, I substitute unsweetened apple sauce. Oh, and espresso powder with dark chocolate brownies is delicious."

# Kitchen Tips & Tricks from the Cozy Queens

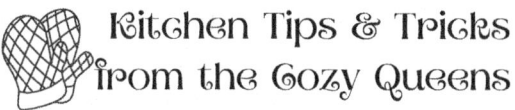

### Ria R.
"I substitute applesauce for oil! It works amazingly well in quick breads, muffins and cookies. But when it comes to brownies. Use oil if you like fudgy brownies, applesauce makes them very cake like."

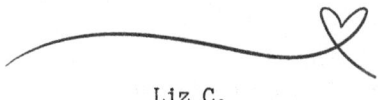

### Liz C.
"When rolling out cookie dough, rather than flour, I use powdered sugar."

### Marcia B.
"I bake bacon rather than frying it. Put a wire rack inside a rimmed baking sheet and lay slices on the rack. Fat drips away from the slices, and no messy spatters on your stovetop! The slices remain flat; perfect for a sandwich or sub."

### Holly M.
"I have a "secret" way of grilling chicken. I microwave chicken pieces until they are almost done, then put them on the grill for the final ten minutes. They appear to have been grilled but stay so moist."

# Kitchen Tips & Tricks from the Cozy Queens

<u>Georgia K</u>
Quiche is a custard-based egg dish. When making a quiche, you want to use approximately ½ of the amount of liquid to the volume of eggs. For example: If using 6 eggs, use 1 cup of heavy cream.

---

Frittata is more of a scrambled egg-based dish. When making a frittata, you want to use approximately ¼ of the amount of liquid to the volume of eggs. For example: if using 6 eggs, use ½ cup of heavy cream.

---

Swap a banana for an egg in baked recipes. It doesn't change the flavor at all.

---

When making a butter crust from scratch, use a blender instead of blending by hand.

---

Double recipes, like scones, that can be frozen unbaked. You can quickly pull out a few at a time when needed.

# Kitchen Tips & Tricks from the Cozy Queens

<u>Katherine H.</u>
"Instead of baking pizza on a pan, then having to wash the pan and scrub off burnt on cheese or crust, toss the pizza onto a piece of foil and curl all four sides up into a makeshift "pan." Place the foil on the oven rack and bake. The pizza comes right up without being stuck and…..no dishes!"

<u>Nancy Wade, author of Meadowood Mystery series</u>
"When baking cinnamon rolls, use a length of white thread when cutting the dough for pin-wheel rolls. Place the thread under the dough, bring up the ends on each side and crisscross - it cuts the dough and doesn't squash your pin-wheel. Simply throw away the thread when you are done."

<u>Stephanie F.</u>
"When making pudding mix from a packet (to either use for a pie filling or to snack on) instead of using milk, use heavy whipping cream and whip with a whisk until peaks form. Let it set. The result is a nice moose-like texture and sooo yummy!"

# Kitchen Tips & Tricks from the Cozy Queens

### Traci A
"Parchment paper! Use it whenever you don't want something to stick to a pain. Cake, bacon, biscuits, most anything. But when you tear off a piece and put it on the pan it won't stay in place - until you crumple it up into a ball and then straighten it out. Then it stays perfectly!"

### Jen C
"When making with dark chocolate brownies, if the recipe calls for oil, substitute espresso powder. Delicious!"

### Stacey S.
"Juice a bag of limes or lemons ahead of time, then store in a mason jar in the fridge."

## Stacey's Simple Smoothies

This recipe was shared with me by my incredible friend and reader, Stacey S about two years ago. At the time, I wasn't sure how much I'd use it. Then, my daughter made the high school cheer squad, and smoothies became a way of life. They don't get much simpler or more delicious than this. AND— making all these smoothies inspired the murder for my 4th Christmas Tree Farm Mystery as Jacqueline Frost!

INGREDIENTS:
- 2 large carrots (peeled and cut into bite-size pieces)
- Frozen mango and pineapple (Or any combination of your favorite frozen fruits)
- Splash of your favorite fresh squeezed juice (lime, lemon, pomegranate etc)
- Half scoop of protein powder
- Sprinkle of beetroot powder - enough to turn it into a satisfying red color
- Cold water
- Peeled ginger according to your preference
- one mini cupcake portion of frozen yogurt *optional

INSTRUCTIONS:
- Blend until smooth - about 2 minutes
- Pour and enjoy

#  And Now

## Recipes inspired by the CHRISTMAS TREE FARM MYSTERIES COLLECTION

In my Christmas Tree Farm Mysteries, Holly White has returned home to her historic New England town of Mistletoe, Maine. She's helping her parents at Reindeer Games, the Christmas tree farm she grew up on, and all is quite merry.

Until the body of a historical society member turns up on an antique sleigh near the farm gates, and the new sheriff sets his sites on Holly's dad as the main suspect.

Six stories in, and this series is going strong, thanks to all the readers who contacted the publisher and asked for it to come back when it was on the chopping block!
THANK YOU!!!

\*

The following recipes inspired by
**Christmas Tree Farm Mysteries by Jacqueline Frost**
TWELVE SLAYS OF CHRISTMAS
TWAS THE KNIFE BEFORE CHRISTMAS
SLASHING THROUGH THE SNOW
STALKING AROUND THE CHRISTMAS TREE
I'LL BE HOME FOR MISCHIEF
A WONDERFUL CHRISTMAS CRIME

# Hot Chocolate

Tired of hot chocolate from the packet? Why not try this delicious alternative from The Hearth?

## Ingredients
- 1 cup whole milk
- 1 cup heavy cream
- 1 square 100% dark chocolate
- ¼ cup semi-sweet chocolate chips
- 1 tsp vanilla extract
- 2 tbsp sugar
- Pinch of cinnamon
- Pinch of chili powder
- Pinch of salt

## Instructions
- Heat milk and heavy cream over medium heat
- Stir constantly and avoid allowing to boil
- Break dark chocolate into small chunks. Add dark and semi-sweet chocolate to the mix and melt completely.
- Add sugar, vanilla, cinnamon, chili powder, and salt.
- Stir until incorporated
- Serve hot

# Toasted Marshmallow Hot Chocolate

Kick your hot chocolate recipe up a notch with some flavored syrup and marshmallows! These easy add-ins will take your hot chocolate game to a whole new level!

## Ingredients

- 1 cup whole milk
- 1 cup heavy cream
- 1 square 100% dark chocolate
- ½ cup semi-sweet chocolate chips
- 1 tsp vanilla extract
- 2 tbsp toasted marshmallow flavored syrup
- Pinch of salt

## Instructions

- Heat milk and heavy cream over medium heat
- Stir constantly to avoid boiling
- Break dark chocolate into small chunks. Add dark and semi-sweet chocolate to the mix and melt completely.
- Add vanilla, toasted marshmallow flavored syrup, and salt.
- Incorporate completely
- Serve hot

## Seven Layer Bars

This long-time favorite holiday cookie recipe makes an appearance at The Hearth every Christmas, and on my table as well!

### INGREDIENTS:
- ½ cup butter or margarine
- 1 cup coconut
- 1 6-ounce package butterscotch chips
- 1 6-ounce package chocolate chips
- 1 ½ cups chopped nuts
- 1 cup graham cracker crumbs
- 1 can condensed milk

### INSTRUCTIONS:
- Preheat oven to 350 degrees
- Melt butter in 9 x 13 pan
- Spread graham crackers evenly over butter
- Sprinkle with coconut
- Sprinkle on chocolate chips
- Sprinkle on butterscotch chips
- Drizzle condensed milk over all
- Top with nuts
- Bake for 30 minutes
- Cool.
- Cut into bars and serve

# Oven Ham & Cheese Sliders

Enjoy this easy, can't-go-wrong, comfort food favorite this holiday season or anytime!

## Ingredients

- Your favorite melting cheese (Swiss, mozzarella, provolone, gruyere, gouda, cheddar etc.) sliced.
- thinly sliced, cooked, deli ham
- mini sandwich buns, ex: Hawaiian rolls
- 1 1/2 tsp Worcestershire sauce
- 1 1/2 tsp Dijon mustard
- 1 1/2 Tbsp poppy seeds
- 1 1/2 Tbsp dried minced onion
- 3/4 cup melted butter

** Swap poppy seeds for sesame seeds, fresh parsley, or parmesan cheese!

## Instructions

- Preheat overn to 350
- prep a 9x13 baking dish
- Mix mustard, butter, Worcestershire, poppy seeds (or alternative) and onion in a bowl
- Split buns and layer bottoms in baking dish
- layer with half ham, then cheese, and repeat
- Put the tops on the buns
- Spread remaining butter mixture over bun tops
- Bake until golden brown (20 minutes)

# Kitchen Tips & Tricks from the Cozy Queens

### Robin S.

"I make baked potatoes in the crock pot. I rub olive oil and salt on the skin, wrap individually in foil and stack them in the crock pot. They are usually ready in about 4 hours on high, or you can set to low and cook all day so they are ready when you get home from work. Best baked potatoes ever."

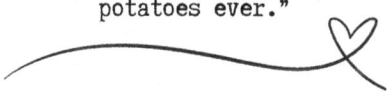

### Jean G.

"Homemade tomato sauce can be too acidic, so I never use sugar in my tomato sauce. I use a Vidalia onion."

I hope this helps

### SHARON W.

To quickly and easily clean any pot, dish or utensil used in making or serving mashed potatoes,
rinse off with COLD water as soon as possible. Potato residue just falls off.

# Kitchen Tips & Tricks from the Cozy Queens

Mary Anna W

"Use mise en place - which means everything in place. Measure all your ingredients before starting the recipe. You'll know if you have everything you need, and ingredients will have time to soften or rise to room temperature if necessary."

---

"If a recipe calls for an ingredient to be soften or at room temperature, don't skip that step. Creaming ingredients like butter and sugar will be easier if the butter is softened, and eggs incorporate more easily at room temperature. Don't even get me started on working with cream cheese that isn't at room temperature. It's a bear."

---

"Making cookies for 1 or 2? Roll the dough into cookie-sized portions then flash freeze them on a cookie sheet. Place the frozen dough balls into a freezer bag & you can easily cook 2 or 3 in a toaster oven when ready."

---

"The only way to truly guarantee a Bundt cake will come cleanly out of its pan is to use shortening & a light dusting of flour. Bundt pans can be incredibly detailed and baking sprays aren't up to the task."

# And Now

## Recipes inspired by the KITTY COUTURE COLLECTION

In my Kitty Couture Mysteries, Lacy Marie Crocker has returned home to her beloved beautiful Garden District in New Orleans. She's opened Furry Godmother, a pet boutique where she makes clothing and treats for animals – much to the chagrin of her high-society mother and to the utter delight of her father and friends.
The homicide detective who continuously finds her at crime scenes and meddling in the investigations is beginning to side with her mother.

\*

The following recipes inspired by:
The Kitty Couture Mysteries by Julie Chase
CAT GOT YOUR DIAMONDS
CAT GOT YOUR CASH
CAT GOT YOUR SECRETS
CAT GOT YOUR CROWN

## Gentle Advisory

- Always consult with your veterinarian before making any changes to your pet's diet.
- These recipes are intended as occasional treats and should not replace your pet's regular diet.
- Be sure to use high-quality ingredients and avoid any ingredients that are toxic to pets, such as chocolate, grapes, raisins, onions, and garlic.
- When introducing new foods to your pet, do so gradually to avoid upsetting their stomach.
- If you have any questions or concerns about your pet's diet, please consult with your veterinarian.

# Terrific Tumeric Doughnuts for Dogs!

Whose doggie needs a doughnut? Furry Godmother has your perfect

## Ingredients

- 1 cup whole wheat flour
- 1/2 cup unsweetened applesauce
- 1/2 tablespoon baking powder
- 1 egg
- 1 teaspoon cinnamon
- 1 teaspoon turmeric
- 1 tablespoon coconut oil
- 1 tablespoon honey

## Instructions

- Preheat oven to 350 degrees F.
- Combine all ingredients in a bowl and mix well.
- Drop dough by spoonfuls onto a baking sheet lined with parchment paper.
- Use a spoon to press dough back and create a hole in the center, or bake in dollops as cookies
- Bake for 15 minutes, or until golden brown.
- Let cool completely before serving.

**Give only as treats and monitor quantity so as not to upset your fur baby's tummy

## Tempting Tuna Treats for Cats

You Kitty King or Queen is just four ingredients and fourteen minutes away from a tempting tuna treat!

### Ingredients

- 5 oz canned tuna, undrained
- 1 cup whole wheat flour
- 1 large egg, lightly beaten
- 2 tablespoons olive oil

### Instructions

- Preheat oven to 350 degrees F.
- Combine all ingredients in a bowl and mix well.
- Roll dough out on a lightly floured surface to 1/4 inch thickness.
- Cut out shapes with a cookie cutter.
- Place treats on a baking sheet lined with parchment paper.
- Bake for 12-14 minutes, or until lightly golden brown.
- Let cool completely before serving.

# Soothing Chicken and Rice for Dogs!

A simple, safe, home cooked dinner for your precious pooch. Because recipes don't have to be complicated to be just what the doggo ordered!

## Ingredients

- 2 boneless, skinless chicken breasts
- 2 cups water
- 1 cup uncooked white rice

## Instructions

- Combine chicken and water in a large pot. Bring to a boil, then reduce heat and simmer for 15 minutes, or until the chicken is cooked through.
- Remove chicken from the pot and shred with two forks.
- Add rice to the pot and cook according to package directions.
- Stir shredded chicken into the cooked rice.
- Serve warm.

# Chicken and Cornmeal Cat Treats

These treats are simple, healthy, and Penelope approved!

## Ingredients

- 1 (5 ounce) can of cooked chicken (in water, drained)
- 1/2 cup cornmeal
- 1 egg

## Instructions

- Preheat your oven to 350°F (175°C).
- In a bowl, combine the drained chicken, cornmeal, and egg. Mix well until a dough forms.
- On a lightly floured surface, roll out the dough to about 1/4 inch thickness.
- Use a cookie cutter to cut out small shapes (or just cut into small squares).
- Place the treats on a baking sheet lined with parchment paper.
- Bake for 15-20 minutes, or until the edges are lightly golden.
- Let the treats cool completely before serving to your cat.

*Continued

# Chicken and Cornmeal Cat Treats

**Variations:**
- add a tablespoon of finely chopped catnip to the dough for an extra special treat.
- For a softer treat, you can add a tablespoon of chicken broth to the dough.

## Gentle Advisory

- These treats should be given in moderation as a supplement to your cat's regular diet, not as a replacement for meals.
- Store the treats in an airtight container in the refrigerator to keep them fresh.

**Enjoy baking for your feline friend!**

# Kitchen Tips & Tricks from the Cozy Queens

### Susy S.

"I have an unusual kitchen tip. I am vertically challenged, so things are often on shelves I can't reach. One day I was trying to reach a can of baking soda, and grabbed the tongs that were sitting on the counter. I discovered that silicone tipped tongs make great grabbers. I have them in multiple lengths from 7 to 15 inches and can't imagine how I got by before (always dragging a chair or step-stool over to reach what I needed). I don't usually grab anything glass, but the silicone will generally hold on to those items fine, I just am extra cautious. My sister-in-law saw me use them one day and was terribly impressed with the idea and has since bought several tongs like mine, since she is also vertically challenged."

### Mary Anna W

"Don't have any frosting available? No time or desire to make your own? Dust or cover your baked good with powdered sugar and enjoy."

---

"Use frozen homemade cookie dough within 2 months"

---

# Kitchen Tips & Tricks from the Cozy Queens

### Mary Anna W

"When making frosting, don't be afraid to beat the living daylights out of it. It becomes smoother & much fluffier the longer you beat it (usually about 3 to 5 minutes)."

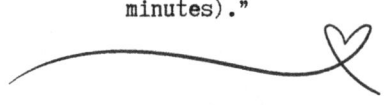

### Stacey S

"Buy unsweetened plain organic Greek yogurt in bulk to save money, then spoon portions into silicone mini cupcake pans. Cover with a freezer bag and freeze. After the yogurt is frozen, pop the servings out and move to a lidded container to free your pan."

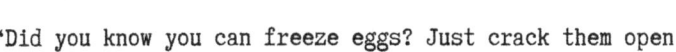

"Did you know you can freeze eggs? Just crack them open into the mini cupcake pan!"

---

"Buy frozen organic fruit in place of fresh for baking. This saves money and eliminates pressure to use before fresh would expire. Bonus: Frozen fruit is conveniently cut into portions appropriate for making smoothies."

## THE BONNIE & CLYDE COLLECTION

Welcome to beautiful, bountiful, Bliss, Georgia, where the days are long, the pace is slow, and shopping can be murder. Visit Bonnie Balfour and her mischievous black cat, Clyde, as they welcome shoppers to Bless Her Heart, their delightful second chance shop on the newly revitalized town square – and help the unappreciative new sheriff solve a local murder or two along the way. Enjoy this recipe from Bonnie's refreshments table and check your pockets before you go, cause her sweet kitty has notoriously sticky paws!

\*

The following recipes inspired by:
The Bonnie & Clyde Mysteries by Julie Anne Lindsey
BURDEN OF POOF
SEVEN DEADLY SEQUINS
BEATING THE WRAP
EYELET WITNESS
FLARED STIFF
ROUGH HEM JUSTICE
STABBED IN THE RACK

# Slow Cooking Barbecue Chicken

Looking for a southern barbecue recipe to wow a crowd? This one is a go-to favorite inspired by the Bonnie & Clyde series. I can totally see Bonnie whipping this together in the morning, then hauling it across the street to share on the square at a community event.

INGREDIENTS:
- 3 pounds of frozen chicken
- 2 cups of ketchup
- 8 Tablespoons lemon juice
- 2 Tablespoons honey
- 4 Tablespoons Worcestershire sauce
- 4 Tablespoons vinegar
- 4 Tablespoons Dijon mustard
- Salt & pepper to taste

INSTRUCTIONS:
- Spray slow cooker with nonstick cooking spray
- Add chicken to slow cooker
- Mix all ingredients in a medium bowl
- Pour over chicken
- Cook on high 8-10 hours

## Sweet Corn Casserole

Need the perfect side dish for your barbecue chicken, ham or turkey? Try this quick homestyle sweet corn casserole and let the compliments roll in!

### INGREDIENTS:

- 4 ounces cream cheese – softened
- ¾ cup milk
- 3 eggs, beaten
- 1 can whole kernel sweet corn, drained
- 1 can cream-style corn
- 1 package (8 ½ ounce) corn muffin mix
- 1 cup shredded cheddar cheese

### INSTRUCTIONS:

- Preheat oven to 375 degrees
- Beat together cream cheese and milk
- Blend in all remaining ingredients
- Spray a 9 x 13 baking dish with nonstick cooking spray
- Pour mixture into dish
- Bake 35 minutes until golden brown

# Blissful Brownie Pie

Brownie. Pie. Need I say more?

### INGREDIENTS:
- 2 large eggs
- 1 cup sugar
- ½ cup butter (softened)
- ½ cup flour
- 4 Tablespoons unsweetened cocoa
- 1 teaspoon vanilla
- 1 dash salt
- *optional: ½ cup nuts

### INSTRUCTIONS:
- Preheat oven to 325 degrees
- Place eggs, sugar, flour, cocoa, vanilla, and salt in bowl
- Beat 4 minutes
- Stir in nuts *optional
- Pour into greased pie pan
- Bake for 30 minutes, or until toothpick placed at center comes out clean
- Cool
- Cut into triangle slices & serve with ice cream or whipped topping as desired

# Cappuccino Pie

A perfect collision of flavors!

**INGREDIENTS:**
- 1 9" chocolate graham cracker pie crust
- 1 3.5-ounce instant vanilla pudding
- 3 Tablespoons instant coffee
- 1 cup cold milk
- 1 12-ounce cool whip (thawed)

**INSTRUCTIONS:**
- Combine pudding mix and coffee
- Add milk
- Whisk until smooth
- Fold in 1/3 cool whip
- Pour mixture into crust
- Refrigerate 30 minutes
- Spread remaining topping over pie filling
- Refrigerate 2-3 hours

# Yummy Chocolate Truffles

Don't deny yourself the decadence of a rich chocolate truffle! Make a batch today!

INGREDIENTS:
- 1 boxed chocolate cake mix
- ½ cup butter (melted)
- ½ cup cocoa
- ½ cup powdered sugar
- 2 teaspoons vanilla
- Several chips of melting chocolate – white or holiday colors

INSTRUCTIONS:
- Bake chocolate cake as instructed
- Crumble into a large bowl
- Using your hands, mix in butter, cocoa, powdered sugar, and vanilla
- Form into 1" balls
- Please on wax paper
- Melt white chocolate chips and drizzle over tops
- Sprinkle with holiday colored sugars, or finely chopped nuts or candy canes

# Banana Bread

Who doesn't love banana bread?!
Try this quick & easy version of a savory-sweet treat!

### INGREDIENTS:

- 3 or 4 ripe bananas (smashed)
- 1 ½ cups flour
- 1 cup sugar
- 1/3 cup melted butter
- 1 egg beaten
- 1 teaspoon vanilla
- 1 teaspoon baking soda
- Pinch of salt

### INSTRUCTIONS:

- Preheat oven to 350 degrees
- Mix butter and mashed bananas in large bowl
- Mix in sugar, egg, and vanilla
- Sprinkle in baking soda and salt
- Add flour and mix
- Pour batter into buttered 4 x 8 loaf pan
- Bake 1 hour
- Cool on rack before removing from pan

# Kitchen Tips & Tricks from the Cozy Queens

<u>Mary Anna Ward</u>
There is nothing wrong with covering a baked good with a dusting of powdered sugar & calling it done. Frosting can take a lot of time & be messy.
Hope these help!

<u>Sharon W</u>
"To quickly and easily clean any pot, dish or utensil used for making or serving mashed potatoes, rinse with COLD water as soon as possible. Potato residue just falls off."

<u>Autum S.</u>
I always had a splash more of vanilla than is asked for. I love vanilla. (It's a great character trait to have! )

# Kitchen Tips & Tricks from the Cozy Queens

<u>Laura S.</u>
"Cream Cheese mixing: Use a mixer and let that do the job of blending the room temp cream cheese that is never soft enough to blend by hand."

<u>Liz C & Beth M</u>
"When rolling out cookie dough, use powdered sugar instead of flour to keep the dough from sticking."

# THE THELMA & LOUISA COLLECTION

A wholesome cozy mystery series with heaping helpings of farm fresh fun!

Welcome to Meadowbrook, a storybook-worthy community where residents enjoy easy, communal living and delectable farm-to-fork treats. The local Polish hen breeder, Louisa Eggers, runs a souffle stand and budding egg enterprise with the help of Thelma, her favorite chicken. She also meddles in local murder investigations from time to time. Much to the chagrin of law enforcement.

Join Thelma, Louisa and the Meadowbrook community on their adventures in these laugh-out-loud whodunnits!

\*

The following recipes inspired by:
The Thelma & Louisa Mysteries by Julie Anne Lindsey
NO FARM NO FOWL
OUT OF CLUCK
NEST IN PEACE

\*

# Overnight Breakfast Casserole

Want a yummy breakfast, but hate waking up early?
Prep this easy meal and cook it overnight!

## INGREDIENTS:
- 1 bag frozen hashbrowns (32 ounce)
- 1 pound cubed, cooked ham
- 1 dozen eggs
- 1 cup milk
- ½ cup of your favorite shredded cheese
- 1 medium onion (diced)
- 1 green bell pepper (diced)
- 1 teaspoon salt
- 1 teaspoon pepper

## INSTRUCTIONS:
- Spray your slow cooker with nonstick cooking spray
- Place a layer of frozen hashbrowns on bottom
- Add a layer of cubed ham
- Add a layer of onions
- Add a layer of diced green pepper
- Add a layer of cheese
- Repeat the layers 2-3 times – end with cheese
- Beat eggs, milk, salt and pepper in a medium mixing bowl
- Pour over crockpot contents
- Cover and cook on low 10-12 hours

Breakfast is served!

# Slow Cooker Ham

INGREDIENTS:
- 8 lb ham, spiral cut
- 2 Tablespoons of brown or Dijon mustard
- ½ cup brown sugar
- ½ cup honey
- ¼ Tablespoon nutmeg
- ½ teaspoon cinnamon
- 1/3 cup water

FOR GRAVY
- 2 Tablespoons cornstarch
- 1 Tablespoon water

INSTRUCTIONS (HAM):
- Spray your slow cooker with nonstick cooking spray or use a liner
- Place ham inside cooker, flat side down
- Pour water into crockpot
- Combine sugar, honey, nutmeg and mustard in a saucepan on medium heat and stir until ingredients melt and combine (3-4 minutes)
- Whisk thoroughly
- Remove from heat
- Pour mixture over the ham
- Slow cook on low 6-8 hours

INSTRUCTIONS (GRAVY):
- When ham is finished cooking, remove from the cooker
- Pour juices from crockpot into a medium saucepan
- Combine cornstarch and water, then move to pan
- Heat until mixture begins to thicken
- Remove from heat and serve

## Creamy Coleslaw

The perfect summer recipe!
Quick, easy, and Oh! So delicious!

### INGREDIENTS:
- 1 bag 16 ounce coleslaw mix
- ¾ cup mayonnaise
- 1/3 cup sour cream
- ¼ cup sugar
- ¾ teaspoon seasoned salt
- ½ teaspoon ground mustard
- ¼ teaspoon celery salt

### INSTRUCTIONS:
- Place coleslaw mix in a large bowl
- Combine the remaining ingredients in a small bowl and stir until blended
- Pour mixture over slaw mix
- Toss to coat
- Refrigerate before serving

# Savory Chicken Crescent Squares

### INGREDIENTS
- 3 oz. soft cream cheese
- 3 tbsp. butter, melted
- 2 c. cooked, cubed chicken
- 1/4 tsp. salt
- 1/8 tsp. pepper
- 2 tbsp. milk
- 1 tbsp. chopped onion
- 8 oz. tube crescent rolls or crescent sheet
- 1/2 c. seasoned breadcrumbs

### INSTRUCTIONS
- Heat oven to 350 degrees. In a medium bowl, blend cream cheese and 2 tbsp. melted
- butter (reserving 1 tbsp.) until almost smooth. add next 5 ingredients, mixing well.
- Separate crescent rolls into 4 rectangles; firmly pinch perforations to seal. If using the
- crescent sheet, cut into 4 pieces with a pizza cutter. Spoon 1/2 cup of meat mixture into
- the center of each rectangle. Pull up the 4 corners, twist slightly, sealing in the chicken.
- Brush tops with reserved tbsp. of butter and sprinkle tops with seasoned breadcrumbs.
- Place on a cookie sheet lined with parchment paper. Bake for 20 to 25 minutes until golden brown.

Makes 4 hot sandwiches. YUM !!

# Kitchen Tips & Tricks from the Cozy Queens

### Stacey S.
"I love smoothies, saving money, and making life easier"
☺
"I buy unsweetened plain organic Greek yogurt in bulk which is way more yogurt than I can eat before it expires. My solution, or hack :) is to use silicone mini cupcake pans. I fill the pan, then cover with a freezer bag and freeze it. Once the yogurt is frozen, relocate to a separate container. The silicone makes it super easy to remove the frozen yogurt."

---

"The same hack can be used for multiple products. How many times have you opened a can of tomato sauce, bouillon, *insert any can or jar of product you only use a bit of for a recipe."

---

"I also buy frozen organic fruit in bags at Costco (any big box store would have similar) which is conveniently cut into portions appropriate for making smoothies."

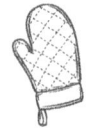  

I hope you enjoyed THE COZY QUEEN COOKBOOK Volume 1!

Whether you took the opportunity to peruse new recipe collections, or revisited some of your favorites, I sincerely thank you for your time. If you'd like to keep in touch and stay up to date with my cozy recipes, series and worlds, be sure to join my [Cozy Queens & Author Dreams Newsletter](), or follow me on social media as Julie Anne Hatcher.

And if you're looking for a new series to try, and you haven't joined second-chance shop owner, Bonnie, and her kitty companion, Clyde, on an amateur murder-investigation yet, I hope you'll make today that day! With names like theirs, what could possibly go wrong?

[The Bonnie & Clyde Mysteries!]()

# Acknowledgments

Enormous thanks to all of my Cozy Queens and newsletter subscribers who shared their kitchen tips and tricks for this cookbook! Your kindness, support and encouragement mean the world to me, and I am ever thankful! In alphabetical order: Reba Anderson, Traci Anderson, Marcia Bellinger, Marsha Karr Cole, Jen Conklin, Ceri Fay, Stephanie Fox-Luehrmann, Carolyn Galizio, Kirsty Gilpin, Jenny Baked Goodies, Ruby Groves, Katherine Holloway, Jean Guido Rachel Johnson, Georgia Karras, Neva Ladehoff, Chris Leathers Royal, Holly Houston Miller, Nicole Peterman, Marti Robson, Ria Rodriguez, Stacey Souther Robin Sweat, Laura Steurer, Autumn Stover, Susy Szymula, Linda Tucker, Jane Ann Turzillo, Cinda Unruh, Nancy Wade, Mary Anna Ward, Sharon Wiseman, and Allison K. Younger

thank ♥ you

**It's been a pleasure cooking with you!**

Made in the USA
Coppell, TX
09 May 2025